D1543686

DATE DUE

How We Get Our Dairy Foods

By Marjorie Ann Banks

Pictures — Lucy and John Hawkinson

BENEFIC PRESS · CHICAGO

Publishing Division of Beckley-Cardy Company

Atlanta   **Dallas**   **Long Beach**   **Portland**

Supplementary

Social Studies Program

How Series

Basic Concepts Series

Photographs furnished by:

The Borden Company
De Laval Separator Company
Richard Surma
National Dairy Council

Library of Congress
Number 63-12763

Dairy foods are an important part of our daily diet. Twenty cents of every dollar spent on food in our country goes for dairy foods. Many machines and people are involved in the preparation of milk, cream, cheese, butter, and ice cream for our tables. Milking the cow is just the beginning step in a long line of processes.

CONTENTS

DAIRY FOODS

Almost every day you eat a dairy food. Sometimes you eat many dairy foods in one day.

You can see dairy foods in many places.
But how are dairy foods made, and how
are they brought to these places?

Dairy foods are made from milk.

Most of the milk we use comes from cows.

But in many far-away places, people get milk from other animals.

A farmer who feeds and takes care of milk cows is called a dairy farmer. His cows are called dairy cows.

There are many kinds of dairy cows.

Holstein-Friesian

Brown Swiss

This cow gives more
milk than the others.

This cow gives
much milk, too.

Jersey

Guernsey

This cow's milk has
a very thick cream,

and so does the
milk of this cow.

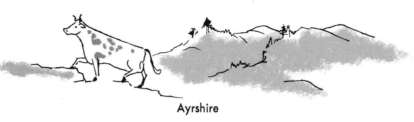
Ayrshire

This is a very strong cow. It can live in
some places where other cows cannot live.

AT THE DAIRY FARM

The place where dairy cows live is
called a dairy farm.

On the farm are many places where
the cows can find good grass to eat.

They eat,

and eat.

A dairy cow needs much water to drink, too.

A dairy cow drinks about this much
water in one day.

In the summer, dairy
cows live outside where
they can eat green grass.

In the winter, the cows
live in the barn. But
what do the cows eat?

The cows eat plants
that were gathered and
stored by the farmer in
the summer.

Loading silo
with plants

SILO

Plants stored in silo

Corn   Clover   Oats   Alfalfa

BONE MEAL

SALT

SOYBEAN MEAL

The farmer feeds his cows other food, too.

13

The farmer and his workers keep
the barn clean and warm.

They keep the cows clean, too.
Clean cows stay strong and give
good milk.

Cows are milked in
the morning,

and at night.

A dairy cow gives about this
many bottles of milk a day.

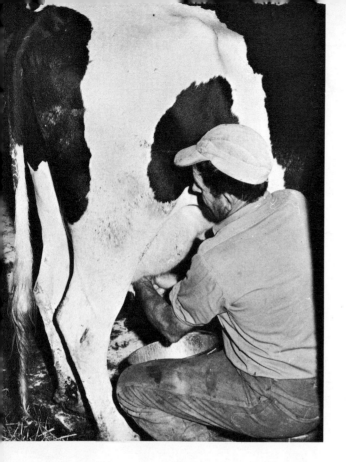

On some farms, the farmer milks the cow.

Then he puts the milk into a machine.

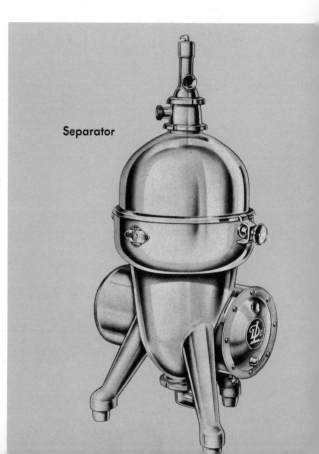

Separator

This machine takes most of the butterfat, called cream, from the rest of the milk. The cream and milk are put into different cans. A truck will take the cans to the dairy plant.

On most big dairy farms today, the cows are milked by machines in a milking barn. The 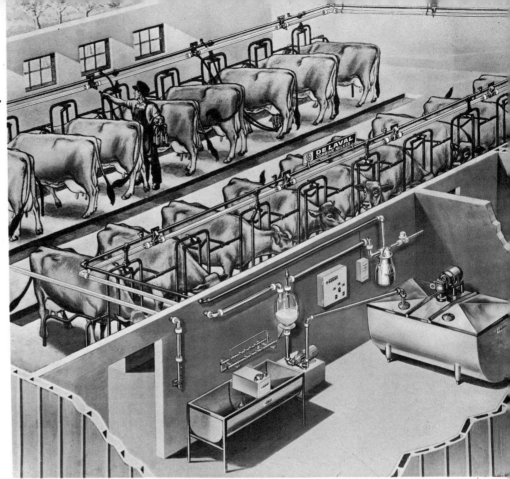 milk goes from the milking machine into a covered can or it passes through pipes into a big tank. The big tank is cold. It keeps the milk cold.

Soon a big tank truck will come and take the milk to the dairy plant.

AT THE DAIRY PLANT

At the dairy plant milk is taken from the trucks.

Men test the milk to see if it is sweet, clean, and without too many germs. The men find out how much butterfat is in the milk. Butterfat makes the milk very good. Butterfat is used to make other dairy foods.

Thick butterfat, or cream, floats to
the top of the milk. Many people
like some cream all through the milk
they drink.

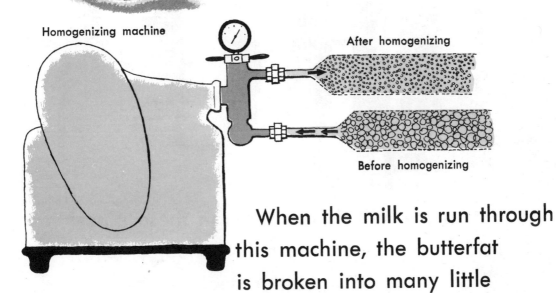

Homogenizing machine

After homogenizing

Before homogenizing

When the milk is run through
this machine, the butterfat
is broken into many little
pieces. These little pieces of butterfat do
not float to the top of the milk.

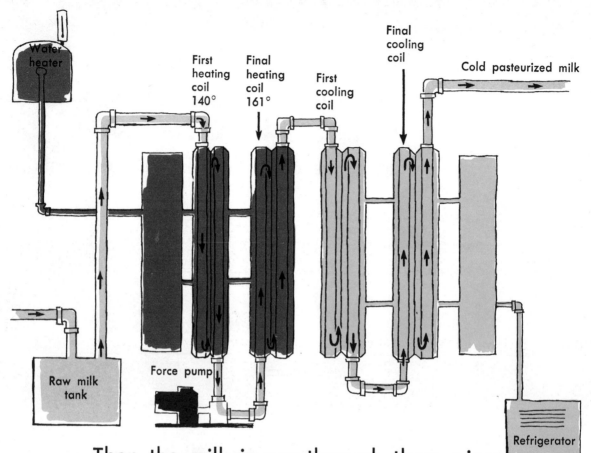

Then the milk is run through these pipes.
Inside these pipes, the milk is heated to
kill all germs. Right after heating, the
milk is cooled. This is called pasteurization.
Pasteurization helps the milk to stay fresh and
good until people can use it.

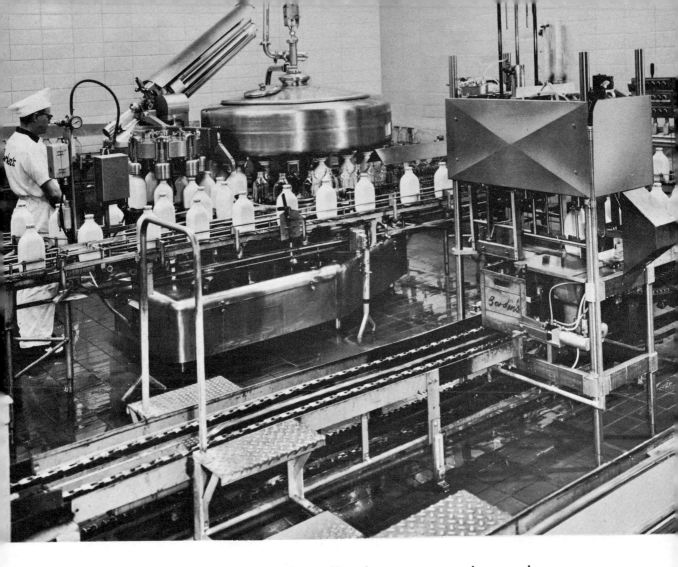

The pasteurized milk then goes through
pipes to another machine. This machine
puts the milk into bottles.

OTHER KINDS OF MILK

Milk as it comes from
the cow is called sweet
milk. Sweet milk can be
changed into other kinds
of milk.

Chocolate milk is a kind of milk
that most boys and girls like.

At the dairy plant, chocolate is put into
the milk. People sometimes make chocolate
milk at home, too.

Buttermilk is another kind of drink that
can be made from milk. To make buttermilk,
most of the butterfat is taken out of the
milk. Then something is put into the milk
to give it a very different taste. Many
people like the taste of buttermilk.

Sometimes much of the water is taken
out of the milk. Then the milk is put
into small cans and heated.

These cans of milk can be sent to places
far away. The canned milk will stay fresh in
a warm place or in a cold place.

Sometimes all of the water is taken out of milk. This is done in these big machines that dry the milk into little pieces. The little pieces are put into cans.

People just put water with this milk when they want to use it. Dry milk can be used in cooking, too.

CREAM

Many people like the taste of thick cream.

They put it on other foods to make them taste good.

At the dairy plant, cream is taken from the milk by running the milk through this machine. Sometimes this is done by the farmer before he sends his milk to the plant.

Worker operating separator

Sometimes people beat thick
cream. They beat it until the
cream is full of air. Then it
can be used on

this,

in this,

or on this.

People like sour cream, too. They use it in cooking and in other ways.

Sour cream is made from fresh cream. The fresh cream is pasteurized and cooled. Then something is put into the cream to make it sour. The cream is then bottled and put into a machine until it becomes sour and ready to use.

MAKING BUTTER

Another dairy food that many people like
is butter. We use butter in many ways.
Can you think of some of them?

People have been making butter for a long, long time.

Used as a medicine

Used on the hair

Used on paper windows to let in light

Long ago, people used butter in food, and they used it in many other ways, too.

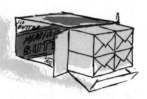

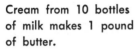

Cream from 10 bottles
of milk makes 1 pound
of butter.

Most of our butter is
made from the cream
of cow's milk.

But butter can be made from the milk
of other animals, too.

Sometimes butter is made in the home or on a dairy farm. But in many places, butter is made at a creamery.

Cream sent to the creamery from the dairy farms must first be tested. Men test the cream to see if it is fresh and clean. They test to see how much fat is in the cream, too. Cream with much fat makes good butter.

After testing, the cream is pasteurized
and cooled. Then it is put into a big tank.

The big tank turns this way
and that. Inside, the cream goes
this way and that, too.

Soon little pieces of
fat in the cream come together
to make bigger pieces of fat.
These pieces are called butter.
The part that does not turn into
butter is called buttermilk.

The buttermilk is taken out of the tank,
but the butter stays in the tank. Water
is put into the tank. Then a worker starts
the tank again. The butter and water turn
and turn in the tank. The turning water
washes out more of the buttermilk. Then
salt is put into the tank. Salt makes the
butter taste good, and it helps to keep
the butter fresh.

The butter is then cooled and put into this machine.

Here the butter is cut and boxed. Now it is ready to go.

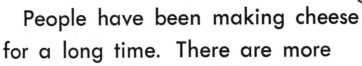

CHEESE

People have been making cheese
for a long time. There are more
than 400 kinds of cheese.

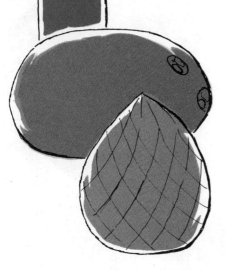

Cheese is a dairy food
made from milk. The milk
is first pasteurized. Then
it goes through pipes from
the pasteurizer into big tanks.

Something is put into the milk to make
it change into a thick part and a watery
part. Cheese is made from the thick part
called curd. The watery part is called whey.

The curd becomes thicker and thicker.
Workers keep cutting the curd into many
little pieces. They keep moving the
pieces around to get all the whey out
of the curd. Heat is turned on. This
helps to take out the whey, too.

The curd starts to stick together.
Workers must cut the curd into pieces. A
machine then cuts the curd into very little
pieces. After this, the curd goes back into
the tank to be salted.

A dairy worker then packs the curd very tightly. This tight packing pushes out all the whey that might still be in the curd. It makes the curd harder, too.

Out comes the tightly packed cheese. Now the cheese must dry. After drying, the cheese is stored away. Every kind of cheese needs a different storing time. In the storing place, the cheese changes taste. When it tastes just right, the worker takes out the cheese and sends it to the stores.

ICE CREAM

Another dairy food that many people like very much is ice cream.

Most ice cream that you eat is made at dairy plants or ice cream plants.

Milk, cream, sugar, and eggs are mixed together to make ice cream. Other things are put into ice cream, too. These things give it a good taste.

41

The ice cream mix is first put into a pasteurizer to kill all germs.

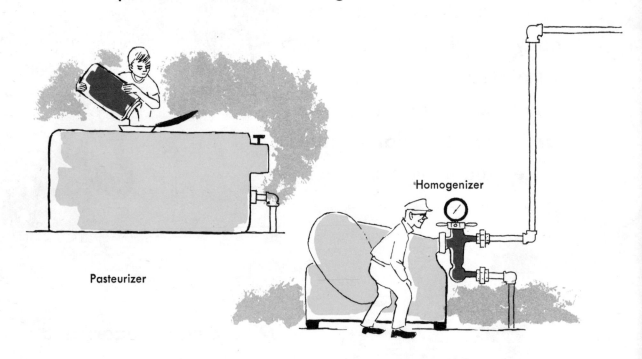

Pasteurizer

Homogenizer

Then the mix goes into this machine. In this machine, the butterfat is broken into many little pieces. This will help to make the ice cream smooth.

The ice cream mix is then cooled and put into a big tank. The mix stays in this tank for a time. Then it goes into the freezer.

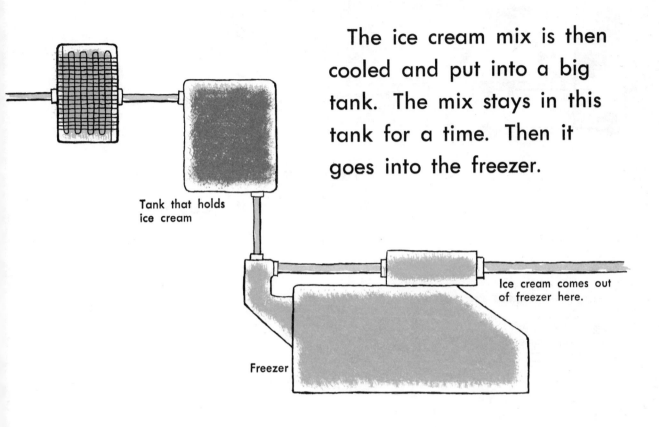

Tank that holds
ice cream

Ice cream comes out
of freezer here.

Freezer

Inside the freezer, the ice cream mix is moved around and around. This helps the ice cream to become harder and smoother. When the ice cream is partly hard, it comes out of the freezer.

When the ice cream comes out
of the freezer, it goes into cans
and boxes.

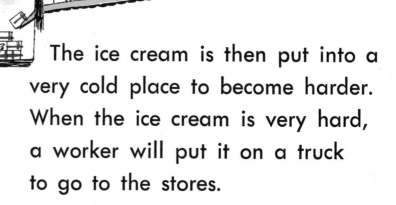

The ice cream is then put into a
very cold place to become harder.
When the ice cream is very hard,
a worker will put it on a truck
to go to the stores.

DAIRY FOODS TO YOU

You can see dairy foods in many, many places. But how do dairy foods get to these places where you can buy them?

Men in trucks like these take dairy foods from the dairy plants and creameries to stores, homes, and other places.

Sometimes dairy plants
send milk and foods by
airplanes and trains.

Dairy foods go by ship, too. Ships take
these foods to people living and working
in far-away places.

Can you see now why many people and machines are needed to make and bring good dairy foods to you?

Dairy foods start with the cows on the farm, but it takes the help of many people and machines to get these foods ready for your table.

Vocabulary

The total vocabulary of this book is 203 words. Of these, 32 are second-grade words, 14 are above second-grade, and the rest are below this level. Second-grade words are listed in roman type, and those above are in italics. The words are listed in alphabetical order, and the numbers indicate the pages on which the words first appear.

beat 27
bottles 15
broken 19

cannot 9
changed 22
cheese 36
chocolate 22
cooking 28
cooled 20
cream 9
creamery 32
curd 37

dairy 5
different 16
done 25

floats 19
freezer 43

gathered 13
germs 18

harder 40
heated 20

ice 41

kill 20

machine 16
might 40
mixed 41

outside 13

packs 40
part 34

passes 17
pasteurization 20
pieces 19
pipes 17
pushes 40

salt 34
sends 26
sent 24
ship 46
smooth 42
sour 28
sugar 41

tank 17
taste 23
test 18
thick 9
tightly 40